# PREHISTORIC LIFE
# DINOSAURS

**JILL FORAN**

**WEIGL PUBLISHERS INC.**

Published by Weigl Publishers Inc.
350 5th Avenue, Suite 3304
New York, NY 10118-0069
USA
Web site: www.weigl.com

Library of Congress Cataloging-in-Publication Data
Foran, Jill.
  Dinosaurs / Jill Foran.
      v. cm. -- (Prehistoric life)
Includes index.
Contents: Special reptiles -- The age of dinosaurs -- A different earth -- Adapting to change --
Finding dinosaur fossils -- Revealing evidence -- Dinosaur detective -- Dinosaur groups --
Dinosaur close-ups -- Growth rates & lifespans -- Dinosaur eating habits -- Disappearing act --
Dinosaur mania -- Still digging for dinosaurs.
  ISBN 1-59036-110-5 (lib. bdg. : alk. paper)
  1. Dinosaurs--Juvenile literature. [1. Dinosaurs.] I. Title. II. Series: Prehistoric life (Mankato, Minn.)
  QE861.5.F67 2004
  567.9--dc21

                             2003003967
                   Printed in the United States of America
                   1 2 3 4 5 6 7 8 9 0   07 06 05 04 03

**Editor** Donald Wells
**Series Editor** Jennifer Nault
**Copy Editor** Heather C. Hudak
**Designer** Janine Vangool
**Layout** Terry Paulhus
**Photo Researcher** Tracey Carruthers
**Consultant** Royal Tyrrell Museum of Palaeontology

**Photograph Credits**
Every reasonable effort has been made to trace ownership and to obtain permission to reprint copyright
material. The publishers would be pleased to have any errors or omissions brought to their attention so
that they may be corrected in subsequent printings.

**Cover**: *Triceratops* skeleton at the Royal Tyrrell Museum (**Royal Tyrrell Museum/Alberta Community
Development**), landscape (**Photos.com**); **Corel Corporation**: pages 1, 9, 15T, 15B, 16 all, 17 all; **Mary Evans
Picture Library**: page 25B; **Breck Kent**: pages 13, 19; **Clarence Norris/Lone Pine Photos**: pages 10, 20;
**Photofest**: pages 24 (**©Walt Disney**), 25T (**© Universal Studios**); **Photos.com**: page 6R; **Photovault**:
page 18 (**Wernher Krutein**); **Royal Tyrrell Museum/Alberta Community Development**: pages 5, 6L, 7L,
14, 21, 22, 23; **Tom Stack & Associates**: pages 7R (**Tom & Theresa Stack**), 29 (**Tess Young**); **Dave Taylor**:
pages 3, 4, 11, 12.

# Contents

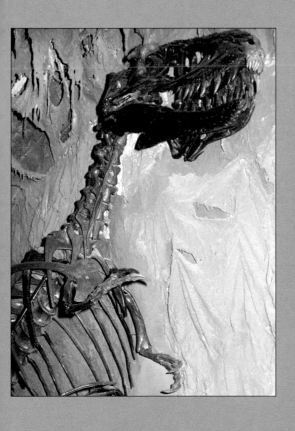

# Special Reptiles

◆　　◆　　◆　　◆　　◆　　◆　　◆

Long before humans lived, dinosaurs roamed Earth. They ruled the world for 150 million years. During this time, some dinosaurs became the biggest and strongest animals ever to walk on land. Dinosaurs became **extinct** 65 million years ago. No one is sure why the dinosaurs became extinct. Even though dinosaurs disappeared from Earth, they were very successful animals that were able to survive many different changes in their **environment**. No other group of large animals has managed to live as long as the dinosaurs.

*Allosaurus* was a large, meat-eating dinosaur. It was the largest meat-eater in North America during the Late Jurassic Period.

*Triceratops horridus* means "horrible three-horned face." *Triceratops* used its horns to defend itself from meat-eaters such as *Tyrannosaurus rex.*

Many types of ancient reptiles roamed Earth when the dinosaurs lived. Some of these reptiles walked on land. Others lived in the sea or flew in the sky. Dinosaurs were special reptiles. What made dinosaurs special was the way they stood and walked. The legs of a reptile are usually attached to the sides of its body. The legs of a dinosaur, however, were under its body. It stood and walked with its legs pointing straight down to the ground.

## DINOSAUR FACTS

- The word *dinosaur* means "terrible lizard."
- Dinosaurs were named in 1842. This was before scientists knew that dinosaurs were not lizards.
- Scientists who study dinosaurs and other ancient life are called paleontologists.
- Paleontologists have identified about 800 different types of dinosaurs.

# The Age of Dinosaurs

♦ ♦ ♦ ♦ ♦ ♦ ♦

For more than 3.5 billion years, Earth has been the home of many types of animals and plants. Scientists have divided Earth's history into blocks of time called eras. The eras have been divided into periods. Different types of plants and animals lived during each of Earth's eras.

## PRECAMBRIAN ERA

Algae **fossils**

### 4.6 Billion to 545 Million Years Ago
♦ During the Precambrian Era, simple life forms first appeared in the seas.

## PALEOZOIC ERA

### 545 Million to 250 Million Years Ago
♦ Paleozoic means "ancient life." During this era, more complex life forms appeared on Earth, including fish, insects, land plants, and reptiles.

Trilobite fossils

The dinosaurs lived in the Mesozoic Era, which is also known as "The Age of Reptiles" or "The Age of Dinosaurs." The Mesozoic Era began almost 250 million years ago. It is divided into three periods: Triassic, Jurassic, and Cretaceous.

Dinosaurs first appeared in the Triassic Period, about 230 million years ago. They **evolved** from a group of reptiles called archosaurs. During the Jurassic Period, 205 to 141 million years ago, new kinds of dinosaurs developed and thrived. By the Cretaceous Period, 141 to 65 million years ago, dinosaurs roamed Earth.

## MESOZOIC ERA

*Tyrannosaurus rex* skeleton

### 250 Million to 65 Million Years Ago

◆ Mesozoic means "middle life." Dinosaurs and birds appeared during the Mesozoic Era. By the end of this era, many of these animals became extinct.

## CENOZOIC ERA

### 65 Million Years Ago to the Present

◆ Cenozoic means "recent life." All types of **mammals** began to appear on Earth during the Cenozoic Era.

Otter-like mammal fossil

# A Different Earth

◆　　◆　　◆　　◆　　◆　　◆　　◆

**D**uring the Mesozoic Era, Earth was much warmer than it is today. In the Triassic Period, the land on Earth formed one large **continent** called *Pangaea*. The climate was warm, the sea level was high, and there was no ice at the North Pole or South Pole. During the Jurassic Period, Pangaea began to divide into separate continents. The climate grew moist, and forests became thicker. In the Cretaceous Period, the land continued to shift and change. The climate was warm, and there were wet and dry seasons. By the end of the Cretaceous Period, the continents looked much like they do today.

## THE CHANGING CONTINENTS

◆ **Triassic Period**
One continent
called Pangaea

◆ **Jurassic Period**
Pangaea begins
to break apart

◆ **Cretaceous Period**
Modern continents
begin to form

# Adapting to Change

Plant-eaters such as *Plateosaurus* had sharp-edged beaks and poorly developed teeth.

The long tail of *Plateosaurus* developed to balance its long neck.

**PLATEOSAURUS**

*Plateosaurus* stood on powerful back legs in order to reach branches.

As Earth changed, the bodies and behavior of dinosaurs also changed. These changes enabled dinosaurs to **adapt** to new environments. The earliest dinosaurs were small. They ate meat and walked on two feet. As more plants and trees became available, large numbers of plant-eating dinosaurs evolved. Then, larger dinosaurs evolved that hunted and ate the plant-eaters. Some plant-eating dinosaurs developed bony armor and horns as protection. By adapting to the changing world, many dinosaur **species** were able to live for millions of years.

# Dinosaur Fossils

D inosaurs became extinct long before humans lived on Earth. It is not possible to go back in time to see them. It is possible to learn about them by looking at their fossils. Most dinosaurs died, and their bodies broke down into simpler parts. Some dinosaur remains became fossils. Dinosaur fossils can be compressions or impressions. Compressions are entire dinosaur skeletons or parts of dinosaur skeletons that were pressed between layers of mud and sand. These layers turned into rock. The dinosaur skeleton and dinosaur parts became fossils. Impressions are marks made by skin and traces of footprints. Impressions are found in **sedimentary rocks** that were once layers of sand, silt, and mud.

The North American badlands have sedimentary rock layers that often contain many fossils.

Most dinosaurs had skin, not scales. Only a few large plant-eaters appear to have had scaly skin. The color of dinosaur skin is not known because fossil impressions of skin do not indicate skin color.

## HOW DINOSAUR FOSSILS ARE FORMED

Paleontologists have found many types of dinosaur fossils. A fossil is created when layers of mud and sand cover the bones of a dinosaur that has died. As time passes, layers of mud build up. The weight of the upper layers of mud pushes down on the lower layers to form solid rock. The remains of the dinosaur become a fossil.

People have been finding dinosaur fossils for thousands of years. At first, no one knew what they had found. Some people thought the fossils were dragon bones or the bones of giant humans. In the early 1800s, scientists realized that the fossils belonged to giant reptiles that no longer existed.

# Revealing Evidence

◆　　◆　　◆　　◆　　◆　　◆　　◆

**E**verything humans know about dinosaurs is learned by studying fossils. By looking at fossils, paleontologists can determine a dinosaur's identity. They can also tell its size and shape. Fossils allow humans to understand how dinosaurs lived. Skull fossils help scientists learn how certain dinosaurs were able to hear, see, smell, and think. Footprint fossils reveal how fast certain dinosaurs ran. Nest fossils tell scientists whether or not certain dinosaurs lived in groups.

No matter how many fossils scientists find, there will always be mysteries surrounding dinosaurs. Thanks to the work of paleontologists, many of these mysteries are being solved.

*Ceratosaurus* was a large meat-eater that lived in the Late Jurassic Period, about 156 million to 141 million years ago.

# Dinosaur Detectives

◆    ◆    ◆    ◆    ◆    ◆    ◆

**B**eing a paleontologist is exciting work, but it takes skill and **dedication**. Paleontologists work hard to solve the mysteries of the dinosaurs. They go on **digs** all over the world to look for fossils. Once important fossils are found, special teams carefully unearth the fossils and protect them from damage. A team of scientists may take many weeks to dig up a dinosaur skeleton. Once the fossils are freed, there is still more work to be done. First, the fossils must be cleaned. Then, paleontologists identify the dinosaur. They compare newly discovered bones with bones from other dinosaurs. They also look at the bones to learn more about the dinosaur's life and behavior. Paleontologists work together to understand how dinosaurs lived. They piece together clues and work from **theories**, much like detectives. Would you like to be a dinosaur detective?

Paleontologists hunt for dinosaur fossils, clean and restore fossils, and teach people about dinosaurs.

# Dinosaur Groups

◆     ◆     ◆     ◆     ◆     ◆     ◆

Scientists have divided dinosaurs into two main groups: saurischians and ornithischians. Dinosaurs are placed in one of these groups based on the shape of their hipbones. If a dinosaur's hipbones are like those of other reptiles, it is part of the saurischian group. *Saurischian* means "lizard-hipped." If a dinosaur's hipbones are shaped more like those of birds, it is part of the ornithischian group. *Ornithischian* means "bird-hipped."

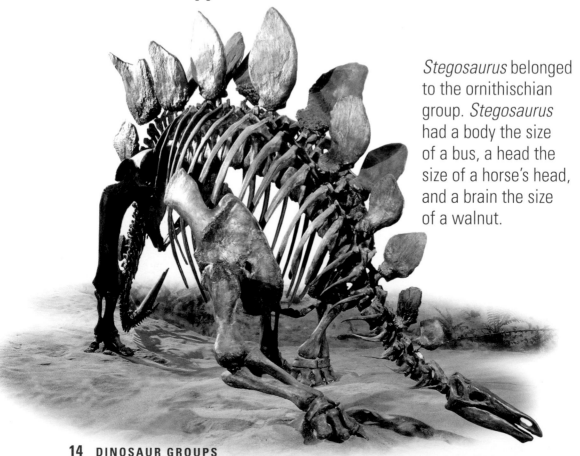

*Stegosaurus* belonged to the ornithischian group. *Stegosaurus* had a body the size of a bus, a head the size of a horse's head, and a brain the size of a walnut.

## SAURISCHIANS: "LIZARD-HIPPED"

There are three basic groups of saurischians: prosauropods, sauropods, and theropods. Prosauropods and sauropods were plant-eaters. Sauropods evolved from prosauropods. Dinosaurs in these groups were among the largest animals ever to have lived. Theropod dinosaurs were mostly two-legged, or bipedal. They were also the only **predatory** meat-eaters among all the dinosaurs.

## ORNITHISCHIANS: "BIRD-HIPPED"

All ornithischians, large or small, were plant-eaters. Ornithischian dinosaurs shared another common feature. None of them had teeth at the front of their mouths. Instead, they had sharp-edged beaks that they used to cut and tear their food. There are five basic groups of ornithischians: ankylosaurs, ceratopsians, ornithopods, pachycephalosaurs, and stegosaurs.

# Dinosaurs Closeup

◆ ◆ ◆ ◆ ◆ ◆ ◆

**M**any different types of dinosaurs lived in the Mesozoic Era. Some were more than 100 feet long, while others were as small as modern-day chickens. Some walked on two feet, while others walked on four feet. Some dinosaurs were fast runners. Others were slow, lumbering animals. There were dinosaurs with horns on their heads and spikes on their tails. There were even dinosaurs with feathers covering their skin.

| APATOSAURUS | PLATEOSAURUS | TYRANNOSAURUS REX |
|---|---|---|
| ◆ Lizard-hipped sauropod | ◆ Lizard-hipped prosauropod | ◆ Lizard-hipped theropod |
| ◆ Lived in the Late Jurassic Period | ◆ Lived in the Late Triassic Period | ◆ Lived in the Late Cretaceous Period |
| ◆ One of the largest land animals to ever exist | ◆ Long neck and very long tail | ◆ Fierce hunter with razor-sharp teeth |
| ◆ Was 70 to 90 feet (21–27 m) long and about 15 feet (4.6 m) high | ◆ Small head with a long nose and jaw | ◆ One of the largest meat-eating dinosaurs |
| ◆ Very long neck and tail and four massive legs | ◆ Large hands with five fingers and a big thumb claw | ◆ Walked on two powerful legs but had tiny arms |
| ◆ Tiny head and small brain | | |

## ANKYLOSAURUS

- Bird-hipped ankylosaur
- Lived in the Late Cretaceous Period
- Weighed about 3 to 4 tons (2.7–3.6 t)
- Thick oval plates on skin and two rows of spikes along the body, large horns on the back of head, and a club-like tail

## TRICERATOPS

- Bird-hipped ceratopsian
- Lived in the Late Cretaceous Period
- One of the largest skulls of any known animal
- Three horns on the face
- Bony plate projecting from back of skull

## STEGOSAURUS

- Bird-hipped stegosaur
- Lived in the Late Jurassic Period
- Had two rows of seventeen bony plates along back and tail
- Four sharp spikes on tail
- Tiny head, with a brain the size of a walnut

## IGUANODON

- Bird-hipped ornithopod
- Lived in the Early Cretaceous Period
- Legs were much longer than its arms
- Could run on two legs or walk on all four legs
- Four fingers and a thumb spike on each hand that was 2 to 6 inches (5–15 cm) long

## MEGALOSAURUS

- Lizard-hipped prosauropod
- Lived in the Jurassic Period
- First dinosaur fossil to be discovered and named
- Large, powerful jaws with sharp teeth

## PACHYCEPHALOSAURUS

- Bird-hipped pachycephalosaur
- Lived in the Late Cretaceous Period
- Large head with solid bone up to 10 inches (25.4 cm) thick
- Largest of the bone-headed dinosaurs
- Bumpy knobs on the nose and the back of the skull

# Life Cycle of Dinosaurs

◆　　◆　　◆　　◆　　◆　　◆　　◆

Like all reptiles, dinosaurs hatched from eggs. These eggs came in many shapes and sizes. Some were small and round. Others were large, long, and thin. The dinosaur that hatched from an egg looked exactly like the adult, only smaller. Some dinosaurs cared for their eggs. Other dinosaurs simply laid their eggs and then abandoned them.

The largest dinosaur egg ever found belonged to *Hypselosaurus*. It was 1 foot (30 cm) long and 10 inches (25 cm) wide. The smallest dinosaur eggs found were only 1 inch (2.5 cm) long and belong to *Mussaurus*.

The femur is the upper leg bone that attaches to the hip in a person. In dinosaurs, the femur is the upper bone in the back leg. A sauropod femur found in Australia was 5.5 feet (1.7 m) long.

Paleontologists cannot be sure how long it took a baby dinosaur to grow into an adult. The time it took for a dinosaur to grow into an adult was probably different for each species of dinosaur. Some scientists believe that dinosaurs developed at the rate of modern-day reptiles. This would mean that a small *Troodon* took about 3 to 5 years to grow to its adult size. A large sauropod, however, may have taken more than 40 years to reach its full size.

Paleontologists use a dinosaur's body size to guess how long it lived. Usually, large animals live longer than small animals. Many paleontologists believe that sauropods lived to be more than 100 years old, while smaller dinosaurs lived much shorter lives.

## BUILDING A NEST EGG

Paleontologists once believed that dinosaurs did not care for their young. The discovery of fossilized eggs in nests shows that many dinosaur parents took special care of their **offspring**. Some dinosaurs built nests to keep their eggs safe. Others covered the eggs with rotting plants to keep them warm. There is even proof that one type of dinosaur sat on its eggs until they hatched.

# Feeding Habits of Dinosaurs

◆　　◆　　◆　　◆　　◆　　◆　　◆

About 65 percent of all dinosaurs were plant-eaters, or herbivores. Herbivores dined on ancient plants such as evergreen trees, ferns, and mosses. They probably spent all day eating just to get enough energy to stay alive. Some herbivores also swallowed rocks called *gastroliths*. These rocks helped grind up the plants in their stomachs. The remaining 35 percent of dinosaurs were meat-eaters, or carnivores. They ate eggs, fish, insects, and other dinosaurs. Many carnivores were skilled hunters. Others were **scavengers**, feeding off dead animals.

Different types of dinosaurs had different kinds of teeth. Plant-eaters had peg-shaped teeth and toothless beaks for tearing and grinding plants. Meat-eaters had sharp-pointed teeth for tearing flesh and crushing bones.

# Food Web

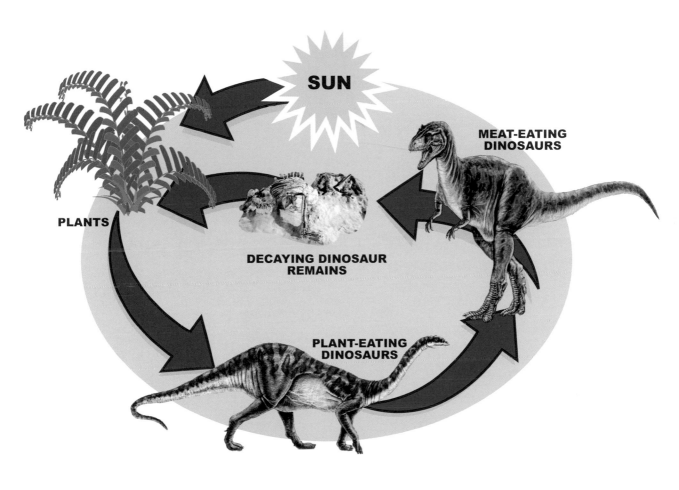

**SUN**

**PLANTS**

**DECAYING DINOSAUR REMAINS**

**MEAT-EATING DINOSAURS**

**PLANT-EATING DINOSAURS**

## FOOD WEB

Just like life today, all prehistoric life relied on an exchange of energy, also called a food web. For the dinosaurs, this food web began with plants. The plants made their own food by converting the Sun's rays into energy. These plants were eaten by herbivores. Herbivores were eaten by carnivores. When a dinosaur or any other living thing died, its body would break down and provide food for plants.

# Disappearing Act

◆　　　◆　　　◆　　　◆　　　◆　　　◆　　　◆

**D**inosaurs lived for about 150 million years. In the Late Cretaceous Period, about 65 million years ago, they mysteriously died. Dinosaurs were not the only animals to disappear during this period. Nearly half the world's animal and plant species also became extinct. There are many theories to explain why these animals and plants died. Some scientists believe the dinosaurs disappeared because they could not adapt to climate changes. Other scientists believe that a huge **meteorite** crashed into Earth and hurled tons of dust into the air.

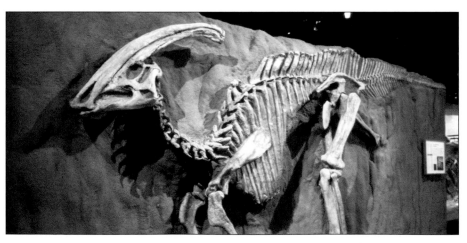

*Parasurolophus* had a hollow, bony crest on the top of its head that could be as long as 6 feet (1.8 m). The crest may have been used to produce sounds or to improve the animal's sense of smell.

Only four **mummified** dinosaurs have ever been found. The most recent one was found in the U.S. state of Montana in 2000. It is the first mummified dinosaur found in 70 years.

The dust from the meteorite crash formed a thick cloud that blocked out light from the Sun. Soon, plants died because they could not get enough sunlight. Plant-eating dinosaurs starved to death. Since there were no plant-eating dinosaurs to eat, meat-eating dinosaurs died, too. In time, all of the dinosaurs died. This theory is popular, but nobody is certain what happened to the dinosaurs.

## AN OLD THEORY OF EXTINCTION

Early scientists once believed that ancient warm-blooded animals, the ancestors of modern-day mammals, were responsible for the disappearance of the dinosaurs. According to this theory, small, furry animals ate all of the dinosaur eggs. Today, this theory is as extinct as the dinosaurs.

# Dinosaur Mania

◆          ◆          ◆          ◆          ◆          ◆          ◆

**D**inosaurs are among the most popular animals in the world. This is amazing because no one has ever seen a real dinosaur. People became interested in dinosaurs in 1854 when the first dinosaur models were put on display in a park in London, England. The display models included *Hylaeosaurus*, *Iguanodon*, and *Megalosaurus*. At that time, not much was known about dinosaurs, and the models had many **anatomical** mistakes. Still, people from near and far came to see the models.

The book, *Dinotopia*, was published in 1992. It told the story of humans and dinosaurs living together on a lost island. A television miniseries of the book was released in May 2002.

Actor Sam Neill played a paleontologist in the *Jurassic Park* movies.

People are still interested in dinosaurs. Dinosaur theme parks, such as Dinosaur Park and Museum in Ogden, Utah, can be found all over the world. Another museum, The Royal Tyrrell Museum of Palaeontology, showcases dinosaur fossils. Located in Alberta, Canada, this museum holds dozens of skeletons and hundreds of fossils. These places are visited by millions of people every year. Dinosaurs have also been the subject of books, movies, and television shows. Children play with dinosaur toys, collect dinosaur pins, and even sleep on dinosaur bed sheets.

## A TABLE FIT FOR A DINOSAUR

Richard Owen and Benjamin Waterhouse Hawkins made the world's first dinosaur models. In 1854, they hosted a dinner party inside a partially completed model of *Iguanodon*. The life-size model was able to hold twenty guests.

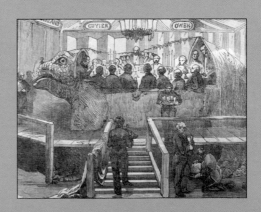

# Digging for Dinosaurs

Since the beginning of the nineteenth century, dinosaur fossils have been found on every continent. Every year, paleontologists make new dinosaur discoveries. This map shows some exciting discoveries of dinosaurs.

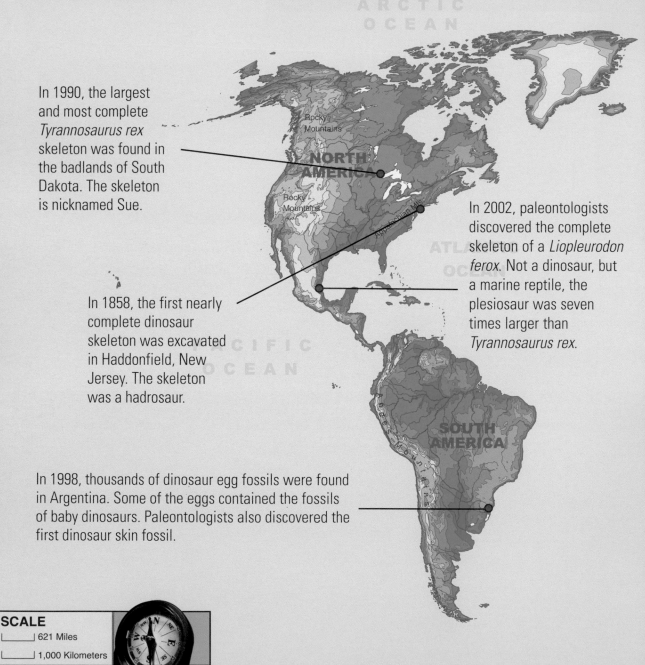

In 1990, the largest and most complete *Tyrannosaurus rex* skeleton was found in the badlands of South Dakota. The skeleton is nicknamed Sue.

In 2002, paleontologists discovered the complete skeleton of a *Liopleurodon ferox*. Not a dinosaur, but a marine reptile, the plesiosaur was seven times larger than *Tyrannosaurus rex*.

In 1858, the first nearly complete dinosaur skeleton was excavated in Haddonfield, New Jersey. The skeleton was a hadrosaur.

In 1998, thousands of dinosaur egg fossils were found in Argentina. Some of the eggs contained the fossils of baby dinosaurs. Paleontologists also discovered the first dinosaur skin fossil.

**SCALE**

| 621 Miles

| 1,000 Kilometers

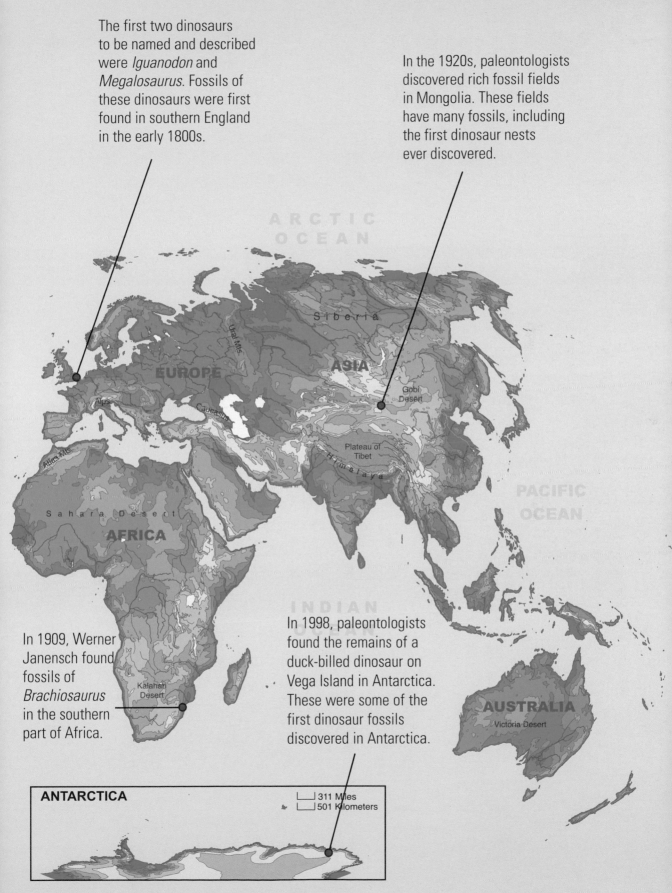

The first two dinosaurs to be named and described were *Iguanodon* and *Megalosaurus*. Fossils of these dinosaurs were first found in southern England in the early 1800s.

In the 1920s, paleontologists discovered rich fossil fields in Mongolia. These fields have many fossils, including the first dinosaur nests ever discovered.

In 1909, Werner Janensch found fossils of *Brachiosaurus* in the southern part of Africa.

In 1998, paleontologists found the remains of a duck-billed dinosaur on Vega Island in Antarctica. These were some of the first dinosaur fossils discovered in Antarctica.

ARCTIC OCEAN

Siberia

EUROPE

ASIA

Ural Mts.

Alps

Caucasus

Gobi Desert

Plateau of Tibet

Himalaya

Atlas Mts.

Sahara Desert

AFRICA

PACIFIC OCEAN

Kalahari Desert

INDIAN OCEAN

AUSTRALIA

Victoria Desert

ANTARCTICA

311 Miles
501 Kilometers

# Further Research

## WEB SITES

To tour a dinosaur museum, visit:
**http://www.tyrrellmuseum.com**

To hunt for dinosaur eggs, visit:
**http://nationalgeographic.com/features/96/dinoeggs**

To find out how to become a paleontologist, visit:
**http://www.paleosoc.org**

For all kinds of fun information about dinosaurs, visit:
**http://www.enchantedlearning.com/subjects/dinosaurs**

## BOOKS

Benton, M. J. *Walking with Dinosaurs: Fascinating Facts*. New York: Dorling Kindersley Publications, 2000.

Burnie, David. *The Kingfisher Illustrated Dinosaur Encyclopedia*. New York: Kingfisher Publications, 2001.

Tanaka, Shelley. *New Dinos: The Latest Finds! The Coolest Dinosaur Discoveries!* New York: Atheneum Books for Young Readers, 2003.

Zimmerman, Howard. *Dinosaurs! The Biggest, Baddest, Strangest, Fastest*. New York: Atheneum Books for Young Readers, 2000.

# Ancient Activity

Nest of dinosaur eggs

**M**ake your own papier-mâché dinosaur eggs that can be hatched. To make your dinosaur eggs, you will need:

- one balloon for each dinosaur egg
- old newspaper and markers
- flour-water glue
- tiny, plastic dinosaur for each dinosaur egg

Mix 1 cup (237 ml) of flour into 1 cup (237 ml) of water until the mixture is thin and runny. Stir mixture into 4 cups (946 ml) of boiling water heated on the stove. Simmer for about 3 minutes, then cool. Tear 1-inch (2.5-cm) strips of newspaper. Place a small, plastic dinosaur inside a balloon, and blow it up. Dip each strip of paper in the glue, and cover the balloon with the paper strips. Use at least two layers of paper, and let each layer dry overnight. Let the egg dry for a few days. When the egg is dry, pop the balloon with a pin, and remove it from inside the egg. Next, decorate it with markers. Whenever you choose, crack the egg open to reveal the baby dinosaur.

# Quiz

♦ ♦ ♦ ♦ ♦ ♦ ♦

**Based on what you have read, answer the following questions:**

1. What are the two main groups of dinosaurs?
2. In which of Earth's eras did the dinosaurs live?
3. Were most dinosaurs plant-eaters or meat-eaters?
4. What are the three periods of the Mesozoic Era?
5. Which two dinosaurs were named first?
6. Which dinosaurs were among the largest animals to ever exist?
7. How were baby dinosaurs born?
8. What are *gastroliths*?

1. The two main groups are saurischians, or lizard-hipped, and ornithischians, or bird-hipped.
2. Dinosaurs lived during the Mesozoic Era.
3. Most dinosaurs were plant-eaters, or herbivores.
4. The three periods of the Mesozoic Era are Triassic, Jurassic, and Cretaceous.
5. The first two dinosaurs named were *Megalosaurus* and *Iguanodon*.
6. The sauropods were among the largest dinosaurs.
7. Like all reptiles, baby dinosaurs hatched from eggs.
8. *Gastroliths* are rocks that some dinosaurs swallowed to help them digest the plants in their stomachs.

# Glossary

◆ ◆ ◆ ◆ ◆ ◆ ◆

**adapt:** adjust to different conditions or environments

**anatomical:** the body structure of animals or plants

**continent:** a large land mass

**dedication:** giving time and energy to something

**digs:** places where soil and objects are carefully removed from an area of historical interest

**environment:** an area in which something lives

**evolved:** changed slowly over time

**extinct:** no longer alive anywhere on Earth

**fossils:** the rocklike remains of ancient animals and plants

**mammals:** warm-blooded animals that give birth to live young, have hair on their bodies, and produce milk for their young

**meteorite:** a body of rock from outer space that has reached Earth

**mummified:** dried up and shriveled due to complete loss of moisture

**offspring:** the children or young of a parent

**predatory:** catching and eating living animals

**scavengers:** animals that feed on the remains of dead animals

**sedimentary rocks:** rock that has formed from smaller rocks and has been compressed over time

**species:** a group of animals that are similar and can breed together

**theories:** ideas that explain an event or fact

# Index